Your Second Fifty Years

∞

Inspiring Ideas for the Second Half of Your Life

∞

By

Doree Steinmann

Published by

Independent Words

Los Angeles, California

ISBN-13:
978-0991603909 (Independent Words)

ISBN-10:
0991603907

Acknowledgements

Thanks to the hundreds of people I have interviewed over the years for the "Your Second Fifty Years" television program, for the generous sharing of their life stories and advice.

Thanks also to the many technicians who over the years contributed to the airing of the program.

My thanks also go to my editor, Donna Wesley Rogers, and my publisher Andromeda Edison at Independent Words.

Doree Steinmann

CONTENTS

DOREE STEINMANN

CHAPTER 1
MY FIFTIETH BIRTHDAY

When I reached my fiftieth birthday, I said to myself, "Fifty years old? I don't <u>look</u> fifty! I don't <u>feel</u> fifty." That was really a dramatic point in my life. I hadn't minded thirty or forty, and I hadn't even minded forty-five! I managed to breeze through those birthdays beautifully.

Then fifty arrived and I thought that sounded like a little, old, gray-haired lady! You see, I was used to the stereotype. I said to myself again, "I play tennis, swim, ride my bike. I'm active physically. In fact, I really feel better today than I did 10 years ago. Both physically and mentally."

So I talked to myself a little bit more: "Okay, I really expect to and may even live to be 100, so actually right now - I'm entering My Second Fifty Years!" (Yes, in capital letters!) And then, 50 didn't seem so old. I realized that if I do have fifty more years to go, there's so much left to do! I have so much to learn, so much work to do, and so much playing to do, and so do YOU, whether you're entering your second fifty years or your second sixty. We all may have a long way to go and much left to do. So the time to start thinking about what we're going to do with these many years we have left is NOW. Science and medicine have given us the quantity of life today, but it's up to us to give ourselves the quality of life.

Long ago I had a friend who said to me "I'm not going to learn how to type because I'm not going to be stuck in a typing job. I want to have my own secretary and be a manager or producer." Well, frankly if I had never known how to type, I wouldn't have gotten the experiences in my life that helped me to move forward.

One of my first jobs was at CBS in New York City as a Studio Receptionist (a nicer name for Page) taking tickets at the door when people came in to watch the CBS radio programs in progress, programs that were "live" in the 1940's. I had been doing this for about a month in my summer vacation from college, when our supervisor asked if any one of us knew how to type. I was the only one to respond and was promptly asked if I would like to substitute for the Studio Building Manager's Secretary while she went on a two-week vacation. After being reassured that my typing didn't have to be perfect, but it would involve just a few things that needed to be typed, I accepted. They mostly wanted someone to screen visitors and answer the phone. So I moved upstairs to a lovely office as his secretary. After the two weeks were up, I moved back down to the studio. Then after another week I was told that CBS was opening their Television Studios in Grand Central Station and they asked if I would like to be the first receptionist there. Again, I would be required to do some "light" typing. I reminded them that I was going back to college in another month, but they still wanted me until they could hire someone else. So I had a very exciting month meeting many famous people and starting my list of "firsts" which seemed to dominate my later life.

I later became the "first" anchorwoman in the Northern California Sacramento Valley, the first women to run a camera "live" and the first woman director of television. But if I hadn't known how to type, some of this might never have happened!

Since I'd been admitting to being 50, some of my students said to me, "Why, you don't look fifty!" They think they're complimenting me, but I answer them very quickly with "Well, what does 50 look like? It has to look like me because I *am* 50. Most people who do look younger than they are won't admit their age and you just think that they're only 40 or so, you don't really know."

I was turned down when I auditioned for a role in a film calling for a "50 Year Old" because I didn't look it! That filmmaker helped to perpetuate the stereotype. We have to shed our ideas about what people should look like at a certain age. I've met some 30-year-olds who seem and act a great deal older then I am. I've also discovered that it's not just keeping physically fit and feeling healthy that keeps you young, but your mind and your attitude about life, and your work can be most important. If you like what you're doing and you're happy about it, if you enjoy the work that you do and the play that you do, of course you're going to stay looking and feeling younger.

A lady I met the other day sighed and said "Oh, I just can't wait until I retire!" So I asked her what she intended to do, and she told me she would like to travel. I nodded my head in appreciation and said, "Then what are you going to do?" She looked at me in surprise and then didn't have an answer. She realized that the travel would be great for a few years, but one gets tired of that after a while and, at 55, she hopefully had so many years left!

So whether you're 32, 52 or 72, you do have many years ahead of you, so you must decide what you're going to do with these years. If you're unhappy or bored with your chosen career, why stay? It would be much more exciting to change careers and do something that you can enjoy. First, start by thinking about what you can do to work your way in to something else without taking a clean break from your present job. Turn a hobby into a career, take some courses at night in a new field, or try something else on the side for a while to develop your confidence.

If you're fortunate enough to have retirement money coming to you, pay can be a very low priority. Maybe you will have a partial income and just want to supplement it. However, most of us want to do something meaningful and interesting and still get paid for it. That's not an impossible thought!

Now I sound like what I have told my four daughters, the old maxim: "Choose something you like to do and the money will follow!" Well, not always, but it's a good place to start, and now in our later years, it's time to do what we like to do. Don't be afraid to take less money as a start, if it's a field in which you have an interest.

Now I'd like to tell you about some real people who have changed careers around the age of 50, including myself, and maybe you can get some ideas from them, and certainly some self-confidence that you're not too old to do the same!

CHAPTER 2
RE-ENTRY PROGRAMS

Back in 1944 when I graduated from high school, you either went to a four-year institution or you didn't go to college at all but right to work! That was it! We never thought about going back to school later the way you can today with continuing education going strong. That was it in those days!

Since I was in New York State, I went to Syracuse University where I was only a C+ student because I was interested in many other things besides my studies: the extracurricular activities, belonging to a sorority, and men! All these took some of my time so my studies suffered, but I graduated with a BS degree in Radio, in the School of Speech, College of Liberal Arts. And I got that piece of paper. It helped me later to become the host of a "Woman's World" daily television program in Sacramento, California, where my husband had been transferred in his job. That evolved into my being the first woman anchor on the "Noon News Report" in 1960. (There were only men in the newsroom in those days!)

I want back to college at California State University, Sacramento, after having four daughters who were now all in school. I really went back just to take a few courses. I hadn't even thought about a Masters Degree. I just wanted to learn a few things, especially about the other side of the camera and skills in the control room of a studio. So I took one course that would teach me some of these things, and I got an A! I took another course and I got another A! (This C+ student here, got an A!) I thought, "Am I any brighter than I was before?" No, the answer was that I wanted to learn what was contained in *that course*! I was interested in the subject and was taking the course because it mattered to me and was teaching me something that I didn't know...and it wasn't required! I wasn't taking it just to get that piece of paper!

I realize that it's very scary for someone going back to school who's saying, "I wasn't that bright in high school, and it's been years since I tried to study anything, so how am I going to do now?"

Well, now that I've been a college teacher, I've discovered that the older students seem to get better grades than the younger ones. Not that they're any smarter, but they're dedicated. They know what they want to do; they know what they want to take; they have a goal in mind, a reason for being back in school; and above all, they're interested in the subject matter. So if you can realize this, it's not as scary as it might otherwise be.

After I'd taken a few courses, I realized that I did want to have some sort of goal in mind, so I went to a counselor and started putting my units together, discovering that I could get a Masters Degree in probably a year. Since I wanted to get into Educational Television (I'd been in Commercial Television for years before), I thought the MA would give me a "foot in the door". Again, that piece of paper would be needed, but with a difference.

In order to get into Graduate School, I had to take a Graduate Record Exam, which would measure me against all other college graduates who had ever taken the exam. Again, here was something scary to me, because it was an unknown. I'd been out of school for 25 years, and here I'd be competing with recent graduates. I hadn't had a math course since high school, although there I had taken Advanced Algebra and was fairly good at math. But I hadn't used it except for balancing my check book and measuring for recipes, so I was really frightened about the math portion of the exam. The language portion didn't really worry me because I felt that I was pretty well-read and English had been my Minor in college.

In preparation for the math portion of the test, I was told to review with an 8th grade math book to remember some of those formulas. Formulas......x plus y? It really had all left me. So I spent several days browsing through the book and then took the all day exam. Believe it or not, my results came out higher on the Math portion than on the Language! That did it. I got into Graduate School!

Again it was a matter of saying, "I'm going to do it, so what can I do to do better on the exam?" and asking somebody who told me to get that 8th Grade Math Book! Don't be afraid to ask questions because it can really help to get you through those scary times.

CHAPTER 3
TEACHING

As I mentioned earlier, at the age of 41, after being in commercial radio and television, I wanted to produce and direct educational television and now I had a Masters Degree with my project (instead of a thesis) which was a "Creative Dramatics" program aimed at 4th and 5th graders. It was used in the local schools for the next ten years. At that time however, the money dried up at the local Public Broadcasting Station where I had hoped to become employed. They couldn't add to their staff.

However, a new Community College was being built with a color Television Studio planned for use by the faculty there and the two other sister colleges that didn't have a studio. A friend suggested that I get a California teaching credential which would enable me to teach there. Since I had minored in English and Drama, the credential came through qualifying me to teach Speech (within my major) and also English, Drama, and Communications to K-14 grades. The latter (Communications) included my experience in Radio and Television, before computers came along.

Teaching? My goodness, that was the last thing I thought I would want to do. I had always heard that "Those who could do, would do, and those that couldn't do, could always teach!" Was I misled! Because teaching turned out to be the most fun and the most rewarding of anything I had ever done!

The college hired me as the Speech teacher and also to produce the television programs on the side. During my one year as the only Speech teacher on campus, I realized that in order to produce my television programs, I needed camera people and others in the control room who were trained in those positions. I got the go-ahead to develop a curriculum in Broadcasting where we could train people in the profession and let them develop their skills while helping me to produce material for use at the three colleges. So I moved on from teaching Speech to teaching all the Broadcasting courses. As the department grew under me into 6 daytime and 8 evening teachers, I eventually became the part-time Department Chair with a Secretary! I didn't need to type anymore, but of course, I still did sometimes. And when computers came along a short time later, I was prepared!

In essence, I created my own job. Although I hadn't trained to be a teacher, I was teaching a subject in which I had had personal professional experience. That counted for so much. Best of all, I really enjoyed teaching. I was imparting my knowledge and experience in the real Broadcasting world to students who were very eager to learn. At the same time, my creative juices were satisfied by seeing what the students produced. I could make suggestions to help them improve. I found this very exciting and fulfilling. I was later gratified when I received letters from former students thanking me for starting them on their careers in Broadcasting.

I really feel that some of the best teachers are those who have experienced their profession first hand, and therefore many of you who have been working in a field for most of your life could then be the one to teach others. There's a special need for people in finance and science to become teachers because they are the ones who know the pitfalls and real life situations and the up-to-date information about the field.

Enough about me. Let me tell you about the real people I have met who are doing exciting and fulfilling things with their second fifty years.

Teaching Construction Management

Robert, 60, was in the Construction business most of his life. His wife, Jean was a Physical Education teacher who recently moved into another teaching career, working with the Physical Handicapped. She had to return to college to earn a Masters in order to work in this very specialized field. So Robert too decided to go for his Masters degree because he thought that he would like to teach also. Today he is happily teaching Construction Management at a California State University.

How about Business Classes?

Some teachers I know are doing just the opposite, ones who have been teaching all their lives and want to take an early retirement to get into the field that they've been teaching. Pat, who taught Business Courses for years at a Community College, has opened her own part-time business as a Financial Planner and is putting to use some of the expertise she has gained in her years of teaching others about financial planning. She expects to retire from teaching soon at the age of 55, and then to spend her full time in her own business.

Volunteer Teaching

Today, there are a number of Professors from a UC near me who teach classes for our Lifelong Learners Association. They donate their time, but they teach us Seniors in separate classes, not for the regular students, just for us. The money we pay for the classes are a donation for us as well, since it goes directly into Book Scholarships for returning students. It's a plus for all of us and then we Seniors get the benefit of learning about something we love or simply want to know to enrich our lives.

A University Professor

One Professor, Michael, 80 years old, a slightly-built gentleman with crinkly smiling eyes, is a very knowledgeable and entertaining teacher. He is English and has a slight accent as he enthusiastically discusses the Shakespeare plays that will be produced the following summer at the University. He talks about how and when they were written, always with his great sense of humor. Although not paid to do it, he loves teaching us Seniors since he is one of us himself, a retired Senior.

Another University Professor

Miriam, 70, a petite, charming lady with curly brown hair, teaches an "Opera" class on Wednesdays for two hours at our local library preceding the Saturday morning performances "Live from the Met" seen at a local movie theatre. In her past, she taught many different languages at

UCSC, French being her original first language and Spanish being her second. She later took Russian so that she could understand many of their operas in the original tongue. Theatre was another love for Miriam along with music, so these were combined into the study of Operas. Then she could enjoy the beauty of the language in these, which now we hear in their original tongue with English subtitles. She feels that music is a marvelous tool for learning languages.

With her classes for us now, we Seniors have the opportunity of learning about the composer and some of the singers we will see, as well as listening to some excerpts from the operas on DVD's. It's a very exciting, cultural experience for us, and at the same time she loves to pass on her knowledge to those of us who appreciate her experience. It's a win/win for everyone.

Aerobics & Swimming

Amanda, a tall, very attractive brunette, now in her 60's, was born in England and came to Canada when she was just a few years old. She met her husband when his brother courted and married her sister. The two men had come to Canada from Italy. Amanda never thought she would have a career beyond being a wife and mother, but once her daughters became older she took a job in the electronics business with mini-computers as a Customer Service person, never realizing that the phone skills she was developing would help her later in teaching. After her two daughters grew up, married and moved away, Amanda and her husband retired and moved to California to be close to their grandchildren. Her second career might have been taking care of her grandchildren, which she does, but she wanted to do something else to earn a little money.

Because she loved the water and knew the benefits of working out daily herself, Amanda first became a Volunteer Aerobics Instructor at the local YMCA, then got her Certification in Safety, First Aid and the Limitations of Seniors so, as a Certified Instructor, she could get paid for teaching them. Starting at the YMCA, she then developed a Water Aerobics program using made-up equipment like milk cartons for weights. Her inventiveness in creating low-impact workouts for older people who can no longer jog or do other things because of limited mobility, makes her extremely popular. She loves her job and her students love her.

CHAPTER 4
WRITING

Writing is a career that you can pick up later in life. If you've been doing something much of your life, write about it either as information for others or to help them by knowing about how you dealt with it. Here I am writing about what I was doing on Community Television for years, interviewing people about their Second Fifty Years!

Here are more of the fascinating people I interviewed.

Bus Driver to Novels

Al was a Greyhound bus driver for much of his life, and he wrote about it sometimes in his leisure. He really enjoyed that but was not able to sell much as magazine articles. He had traveled a great deal in the Western US and visited some interesting places while driving the bus, so at 55, when he had saved some money to live on, he decided to give up his job and give himself two years to make it as a writer of Western novels. He didn't sell a thing for a year and a half, but then finally sold his first one. After that, it was much easier. He discovered that once he had sold his first novel, several of his earlier ones were purchased as well. He did find that he would have to sit at that typewriter, or computer today, for about five hours each day and make himself write, even if the thoughts didn't come. He felt he had to dedicate a lot of time to the writing and found he couldn't do it while having a full time job.

His wife had written mystery stories, so the two of them would sit together writing each day and when they would travel they would take their computers along to keep up their routine. Al feels that writing can be learned and is not an inherited quality because he, his wife and their daughter (who is writing now as well) all learned how, and (I'm quoting him) saying, "We each had a different set of parents." He feels that it's a good second career but that sometimes we have to sacrifice a little by giving it a chance, if you have enough money to live on. But give yourself a goal as he did, giving himself two years to make it. He's now making a very good living with his writing.

News Reporter to Travel Writer

I know two lovely women in their middle life who quit their jobs writing for a newspaper and decided that they wanted to see the country, so they sold all their possessions and bought a motor home. They spent a year traveling, writing in their own journals as they went and are now writing about their experiences in magazine articles. There were many interesting things they ran into, two women traveling alone. They discovered that they both had a great sense of humor, so most of it is very funny! Now they are interested in turning their true life situations into a television series.

Five Women Writing Together

Fifteen women in my town had a club reading Mystery Books and at one meeting when they discussed a book, they all agreed that it was terrible. "Even we could do it better", said one and that started it. Several of the women were writing their own books at the time so they dropped out and several others had too many commitments and were too busy, so the group ended up with five of them who wanted to work together on a mystery.

They chose a location they all knew locally and started in with a heroine. They cut out pictures from magazines to decide what she would look like, so they could all picture her while writing, and they started with a murder! From there on, they met monthly around different dining room tables and later more often as needed. They delved out certain chapters to a member to work on and decided on one person to gather all the writings.

So it began and it took them five years, but they finished and self-published their first book. They knew someone who had some experience in publishing and could format their writing, so that helped. Since it was written locally where they lived, the bookstores invited them for signings and the publicity was so great, they sold a huge number of copies. People loved reading about the local places where the story took place and recognizing them.

A year later, the women missed their meetings together and decided to write another book with the same lead characters. Two of their members were ill but wanted to continue, so they decided to meet more often. Since they had the knack of working together, this second book only took them five months.

I asked if all of their husbands were supportive and one laughed, "What husband isn't delighted to have his wife absorbed in something each day and to meet with her friends to discuss it?" They told me that all the husbands were very pleased and some even made some suggestions. Since the two ill members have passed away, they nixed writing any more books, but are on to other things in their retirement. One is designing clothes from old discarded cashmere sweaters and another is painting water colors of scenes around the town. These women just can't sit still!

Writer on a Chicken Bus

"Adventures of a Chicken Bus Kid" sounds like an intriguing name of a book being written by my friend, Doreen. In 1951, as a bright, chipper graduate from a University and newly divorced, she couldn't find a job, so decided to move to Mexico where she was told there were many Americans, a good place for artists and there was also a lot of English-speaking Theatre. She started her own troupe with improv's and scenes right in the center of a restaurant. So she got free food. When her son came down they toured Mexico first by bus and then by hitchhiking. They stayed in inexpensive hotels, ate from the street people and never got sick. She loved the jungle where she stayed with a friend for a short time. Finally she decided to get a backpack and travel all over South America by herself.

She traveled for years in Guatemala, where she got some part-time jobs and even stayed with a family to help with their children. As she traveled, other people would put her up for the night. Running out of money in Costa Rica, she went to San Jose where she worked telling fortunes. Then she went to Ecuador where she worked as a Clown. She lost all of her money there and she suddenly realized that she could teach English at a local University. She tutored students for a while until they went on strike. She kept a journal all along of these adventures, doing all this traveling on hardly any money! She finally came back to New Mexico to get a Masters Degree, teaches English as a Second Language and has been doing that ever since. And now she is writing a book about her wonderful adventures on a Chicken Bus!

Reporter to Novelist

Betty, a very sweet-looking lady, seems very quiet until she starts talking about writing. She got the "Best in Class" award in a high school Creative Writing class, but then she was busy raising 6 children for a number of years. Later she became an Editor at a newspaper for a law firm and worked on several other small newspapers. She even worked as a reporter for while. She edited the "Labor Union Gazette" for about 5 years and then worked on "Construction Labor News". Then recently, she decided to write a novel. She was tired of factual writing and wanted to do something from her imagination. Her fifth novel finally got published by a small affiliate of Random House as a print-on-demand book.

A reviewer of Betty's book said, "It's so nice to read a novel that doesn't have a lot of sex, violence and foul language, especially with an ending that is a surprise!" Betty believes that we should write about things we know, so she chose a condo belonging to a friend, not her own, to set the scene. However, she visited it often to make it authentic. She also used some famous people in the novel, like David Letterman, who supposedly interviewed the parents of the first child born in the Millennium (the name of the book) and Katie Couric. Since they are considered in the "Public Domain", Betty confided, it is okay to mention famous people as long as you don't do it in a derogatory way.

She has just started on a sequel to this book and is working on a deal to publish her other four, since she has received good reviews from several newspapers and has sold copies around the world. Getting one book published with a good response sometimes opens the door to others you have written or might write in the future. Especially today with all that is happening on the Internet.

Publisher to Author

Jim, a tall, slender, husky-voiced man, became a first-time novelist at the age of 82. Sometimes it takes a while, but we older people have a lot of stories to tell! He was in the textbook publishing business for over 40 years in New Jersey and worked with several well known publishing houses. He came to California because his grandchildren lived there. It was then that he decided to write a book called "My First Murder". Since he lived near the beach, he decided to start with a body found on the beach, a man who probably jumped or was thrown from the cliff above. He went from there. He finally found the same publisher as Betty (above) and was very successful. He has another book he's working on going back to 1934 and a second one taking place in New York City where he used to work.

When I asked him if he sat down at the computer to write each day, he surprised me by saying, "No". Between delivering Meals on Wheels to other Seniors and going to the doctor for him or his wife, it's usually after dinner that he sits down for about an hour to write. During the day, however, some of the ideas are in his head, he says, and he knows that when he gets back to the computer, he can write them down. Completely opposite from other writers I've talked with. We're all different, and whatever works for you is great!

Lastly, before I left him, he told me that he's now writing a book about "How to Write a Mystery Book" so we can take some of his advice. He says, "Let it flow. Get your characters in mind and new ones may come in. Relationships will then develop. Solve them as they go along and use your imagination. When you have 5 choices as to how it happened, choose one. Have no ending in mind but be flexible, and try a twist in the plot."

Since none of the local bookstore would allow him to hold a signing because they didn't have any books to sell, he asked his friend in a Liquor Store if he had ever hosted a book signing and he said that he had once and would be willing to try again. It was a big success and they got a number of people into the store, which made the owner happy of course, and in the end sold a good number of copies.

Writing About Your Past

Eda, who speaks very slowly with a slight European accent, wrote about her life in Europe before she came to the United States. Her children didn't seem to want to hear her stories, so she decided that someday they might want to know and by writing about it, they could finally read it someday. She started writing mostly for her children in a kind of stream of consciousness, never thinking that it would be published. She called it "Escape from Antwerp: from Terror to Paradise". However she did get several local bookstores to carry her book as long as she provided several copies to them. She had a teacher at a Community College design her cover and she printed a number of paperback copies. A happy ending for her and someday the future generations of her family will have this unique testament.

Teacher to Peace Activist

Donna, a very prim-looking blonde until she opens her mouth to reveal a very warm personality with a pleasantly low voice, majored in Psychology in college after starting out wanting to be a medical doctor. Many of her family had been in the Medical field, but she also enjoyed writing and loved to read, especially short stories. She married and had four boys under the age of five when she wrote her first children's book. Before she could try to get it published, she lost the first page and found it too difficult to replicate it, so she gave up. After the boys were all in school, she got a divorce and decided to go back to school herself and earn a teaching credential. She taught for a while but was unhappy with the bureaucracy of the school and quit. What to do? She carpeted her garage, opened the door and started classes for children with dyslexia. Her medical background helped and she did that for fifteen years. She was very successful in this and is proud that tests showed that she brought these children two years ahead in school.

She then went on a walking trip in Greece and met a women who invited her to walk with a group of 1200 people from Los Angeles to New York and then to Washington DC for Nuclear Disarmament. She was asked by a newspaper to keep a diary and write about the trip in 1986, and she did.

Four hundred people made the trip and, picking up other people on the way, they ended up with fifteen thousand walking into the Capitol. She walked during the next four or five years with several other groups, including Peace marches. She gave talks as a Peace Activist for awhile.

In 1988 she visited Mexico and bought a house there. She met a man from her past life, they married and moved to California to live on a farm where she started growing things and became "sort of", she says, a food expert. When that marriage ended, she decided to write a book about all her adventures, called "Tell Me a Story" with a compilation of all the short stories she had written during her life. It was a memoir for 35 members of her extended family. Everyone loved it so much that she started getting orders from outside her family, so she placed it on Amazon and it can be purchased there.

Then she found a number of stories she had written on her Peace march in Russia and put them together in a book called "Walking for our Lives". She and a friend toured book stores with this book and had signings going on for her there. Note to authors: Donna has to have copies with her to sell, and although this book can also be found on Amazon, the stores want her to have copies there to sign and leave with them afterwards.

A Widow's Journey

Gilda, a pretty, white-haired lady, had been a teacher but retired from that when her husband of many years passed away. She was feeling so lonely that she decided to take a writing class and there started writing in long hand "from the gut" as she says. She wrote about her feelings and the grief she felt about being alone. Her teacher asked to see some of her writings and encouraged her to write some more. She hadn't thought about a book, just wrote different short essays. It seemed to help her through that first year of being a widow. Then someone suggested that she put them together in a book, maybe to help others. So she self-published "A Widow's Journey" and found some success with it. So if you write what you know and feel, it can be very cathartic. And maybe it will help others in the same situation, whatever it might be.

Winemaker to Writer

June and her husband owned a winery in California, and when they retired they sold it and decided to live near the ocean. Her background had been in writing, but with owning a winery and raising a family, there was enough to do there. When they moved however, she contacted a local newspaper to see if she could write some articles for them since they had just lost their travel editor and she had done a lot of traveling. This led to some articles on wine as well, so she started writing about Women in the Wine Industry, calling it WOW, "Women of Wine". She did this until they decided not to pay any more freelance writers, so she turned to three on-line websites for which she is writing today, twice a month. She has also been hired to write for her local Conference and Visitors Council and the Mountains Winegrowers Association. She has received a number of honors, from the National League of American Pen Women and several others. So in writing, one thing seems to lead to another and she has been very busy doing and loving it!

Playwriting

Those big, wide glasses hide a dynamic but soft-spoken woman, Gloria, who wrote many short stories and later decided to try playwriting because it would be fun to see her writing "come alive" on stage. So she took a few courses and her first play was about a Mexican boy she knew who had written her several years later when he was 21, telling her about some of his experiences. She realized that dialogue was easy for her to write and knew it was the "way people speak". She decided to take advice from her teacher to read other plays, not worry about "how to" books. Now she has had a number of her plays produced locally.

Another Playwright

Wearing an open-collar shirt, white-haired Sam was very relaxed as he told me about his career in Advertising and Broadcasting with ABC in New York. He was writing continuously in fiction, but discovered that he had a talent for dialogue. He wrote his first novel in 1966 but couldn't seem to get any others published. He then heard from a teacher that "Reality is the springboard into fiction". So he started from hearing two lines of dialogue on the street and wrote a play that he imagined about those two characters, what might have happened before and after. He submitted it to a local drama group that took new writer's plays and his was featured in one of their play reading sessions with scripts in hand. Local actors loved doing this and it helped the playwright to see how it would look actually produced. Feedback from the audience was very helpful as well. Now he is encouraged to keep going and has decided to do more. After all, he says, what else would he do all day?

A Knack for Dialogue

Pat, a very sweet, heavy-set lady with a large smile, was in this same group and she too had written short stories, but it was her son who was a Drama major at college who suggested that she write a play. She took a class and found that she enjoyed it and had a knack for dialogue. It came very easily to her. Her husband was in the beginning stages of Alzheimers and required her presence most of the time, but when she sat down to write, he left her alone and seemed to sense that she needed privacy. This was a relief for her from her care-giving time. She managed to write a number of plays and the audience loved them. She loves working with various age groups, since she discovered that everybody loves theatre!

Chapter 5
POLITICS

It's never too late to get into Politics, even at the age of 70! I met my partner Bob, a soft spoken, gentle person, after his wife had passed away. He was with me one day when a friend came by to ask me to run for the Community College Board of Directors locally, since I had taught at a Community College in another city. I told him "no" because the only thing I hated while I was teaching and being the Department Chair was the Board meetings. So why in my retirement should I do something I hate?

Then he turned to Bob who was with me that day and asked what he had done before he retired. Hearing his background in finance, he told him that our city needed a Treasurer and that he would be perfect for the job. Bob and I both told him that we didn't know anything about running a campaign and that would be what he would have to do. Our friend told us he would help since he had some experience there. There's always someone around who can help, remember? So Bob ran for Treasurer, and we did all the knocking on doors and letter writing that we were supposed to do and he won! Later he decided to run for City Council, reasoning that as Treasurer he could only give them advice, but as a member he would actually have a vote. He was a shoe-in for the City Council and then became the Mayor for a year. This was a new brand new career for him, all after the age of 70 and he loved it!

One of the Deans at the college where I taught decided that he would like to run for City Council since he could then wield more influence in the area of education and could still keep and work at his college job. So he ran and won and after that became very interested in other political offices.

Volunteer First

A friend of mine, when I was working in Television, decided to volunteer to help a candidate for Governor and that led to a paying job when he was elected. She has been able to follow him ever since as he took other government jobs and she loves it! Another friend who was a nurse became very interested in some of the issues that arose concerning the medical profession. She ran for County Supervisor and won. Now she is considering running for a higher office. There's sometimes no end to that!

Do What Your Husband Did

Carol, a very attractive blonde woman who was an Art and Music major in college, married and raised her family before deciding she would like to do something more. She realized that she wasn't professional enough to make a career with her music and art. She enjoyed both but didn't feel her talent was strong enough in those fields to make a living. Since her husband was an attorney, she started working in his office to gain some experience. She became very interested in law and decided at the age of 50 to go back to college to get her law degree. A month after she passed the bar, her husband passed away. At this point she could have earned her living as an attorney but started teaching at her former law school instead. She says she found that more rewarding.

Later, as she was about to retire from teaching, she was appointed by the Governor to fill a vacancy and became a judge in the Municipal Court. So in her second fifty years, she is able to perform a service in the courtroom. She loves to ski and jog, but also learned late in life to drive a motorcycle. Her advice to all of us is to overcome elements of risk in your life. She certainly did so by going to law school at age 50. And she says she was frightened when she first rode a motorcycle but got over it and now loves it.

A Senior Legislator

Bud, a short, very intense person of 68 years with a background in teaching and working in education in various capacities in his early life, now volunteers as a Senior Legislator in the California State Senate. He goes to Sacramento with 117 other people from different counties to work at legislation to propose bills that have to do with Senior issues. Every fall they discuss the problems that have come up during the year, then vote on their priorities and the top ten are printed up. They take these to their legislators in hope they will author them or co-sign and, of course, vote for them. These Senior Legislators are elected by the locals in their area for this job, and they get a portion of their expenses paid for. Bud enjoys doing that, but he also recently ran for the School Board in his District and won. Serving others seems to be one of his goals.

Another Senior Legislator

Chuck, 73, a tall, rather dashing-looking man, is another Senior Legislator in the California Assembly. His background is in Journalism and he eventually owned his own Advertising Agency. In his retirement he has been writing a bi-weekly column for a local newspaper about Senior Issues. Because he writes his column, he gets many letters and calls locally from Seniors with problems and works to send them to the right agencies for help.

Chuck is a member of the Senior Commission and various other Senior Groups, all of them as a volunteer. Then he travels to Sacramento, as does Bud, and talks with some of the 80 Assembly members of the Legislature. He is Chair of the San Francisco Bay Caucus and so meets regularly with them to decide on proposals to be offered that Fall. He doesn't consider himself to be a politician, but they really do "lobby" the legislators, he says. He also makes speeches locally or talks with some of the groups that he attends to be appraised about any problems, such as places along the sidewalks that are difficult to traverse with a walker or a wheelchair. He keeps his eyes open for scams on Seniors and reports them. Again, he is serving his community, which he says is very fulfilling.

Chapter 6
NON-TRADITIONAL JOBS

Don't fail to look into non-traditional jobs. There are many opportunities for men entering the secretarial field, nursing or elementary school-teaching that were dominated by women in the past. For women, the male dominated fields are now looking for you. There are opportunities and many blue-collar fields if you like being out-of-doors and/or have a little math and science background.

Doing a weekly radio program in Sacramento called "Welcome to my World", I interviewed a number of men and women who were working in non-traditional jobs. Men are working as nurses and secretaries in record numbers and women as carpenters, plumbers and electricians. We are seeing more women as news anchors on television, a career I suffered through the pains of as being a "first". The armed services are also a place for women to join and hopefully to move up the ranks, even recently given permission to go into battle.

Librarian to Truck Driver

Take Janet, who's been a librarian all of her working life. She's 55 years old and is taking an early retirement because she's going to become a....truck driver! She has always liked big trucks, thought they were very interesting, but she'd only driven a small pick-up. Having been around books all her life, she'd read about this vast country of ours but hadn't been able to travel very much. So when she started thinking about another career and being a little worried about the economy and the status of librarians in the financial scheme of things, she decided she'd better start looking around. She took a six-week course in driving trucks and for the next six months will be driving with an experienced driver, before being given her license. She's very excited about doing this and now has a new and very different career.

CHAPTER 7
CREATING YOUR OWN JOB
OWNING YOUR OWN BUSINESS

If you've worked for someone else all of your life, it may be time to strike out on your own for your second fifty years. Your hours in some cases can be your own, but many people seem to feel that even though you work harder, there's more satisfaction because it's all yours!

A Dream Job?

Claude was an electrician and his wife Claudine a school teacher. They always loved sailing so when they retired at age 65, they built a 58-foot ketch and now run a Charter Service in the Tahitian Islands. That is their dream come true!

Sammy was a pilot for years and now owns her own company at an Executive Airport where she rents planes, teaches flying and runs the business that she knows and loves.

Avocation Becomes Vocation

Laura, a tall, slender redhead spent most of her working life in the hearing aid business with her first husband. After he passed away, she knew that she wanted to do something in acting, which she had loved as an amateur. At age 55, she discovered that a local theatre was for sale right behind a large hotel, so she sold the hearing aid business and bought the Playhouse, giving herself the chance to act in most of the productions.

Since she knew many other actors in her city, she started a regular company and put on comedy plays all year round. Having a regular stable of actors she could count on to work for nothing was important because she had to pay the directors and set designer from the ticket sales. She eventually married one of the directors, so together they turned it into a non-profit company and kept it going for almost 25 years.

Find a Need

Carolyn, an attractive brunette of 66, had been a housewife, mother and hostess for her husband when he was in the military, and after he died she wondered what to do with the rest of her life. So she went back to college to finish up her B.A. degree, went on to a Masters Degree in Humanities, still not sure what she would do with it. But it kept her busy and interested. She then discovered that many of her friends who were professional people or who already had their degrees wanted to come back to college to take a course now and then, not especially for credit, but just to learn about something. Maybe they were going to visit France and wanted to take a course in French for Travelers, or maybe they were attending the Symphony every season and wanted to know a little more about the composers and music planned for that particular season, or learn about the artist whose works were being shown in the Art Gallery locally or at a nearby city.

So Carolyn decided to start a series of mini-courses for those people, which would be a self-supporting program at her University. Some of the teachers would volunteer to teach these courses as a donation to the University. She proposed that the group would charge $60 for the year during which people could attend any or all of the courses offered (about 10 different ones). The University liked her idea and hired her to run the program and it's become a great success. She actually created her own job!

Sell Other Artist's Art

Dorothy, now in her late 60's, had been an Elementary Teacher during the early part of her life and had also traveled a great deal with her military-career husband. She always enjoyed painting as a hobby and became quiet proficient at it. But she also realized how difficult it would be to sell her paintings. However, she also realized that if she could open an Art Gallery, she could sell hers along with other artist's paintings. In looking for a place to rent, she ran across an old house which was being remodeled into a Restaurant with shops, right along the highway by a nearby beautiful river in Oregon. She opened her gallery there and it has grown into a Gift Shop as well. She and her artist partner have gained quite a reputation in the area as having very unique gifts.   As a bonus, Dorothy has a great time going on buying trips now, even though her retired husband says that she uses up her profits in acquisitions. But she's very happy and loves her work.

Cook to Caterer

A friend of mine loved to cook and give parties, and she was very good at it. While she was mothering several children, this was enough, but after they went off to college, she didn't want to create for just herself and her husband. So she opened up a catering business, starting with parties given by friends who knew her talents and later deciding to expand and advertise. Now at 58, this charming go-getter has to hire help each time she runs a party.

Stay At Home Job

Lin, an athletic-type of women with soft brown hair and a very willing smile, wanted to be a stay-at-home mom to her boys after her divorce, but she still needed to work. Realizing that she was good with her computer, she decided to teach herself to design web sites. Then a friend who owned a store and had a web site already, asked her to maintain and fix the one she had. Reluctantly she agreed and made herself learn more about this, including adding a shopping cart on the site for this friend. She found that the company who had done her friend's web site had not renewed the domain name as a "dot com" and now she would have to use "dot net" which was not as desirable. Lin taught herself a new skill in the managing of domain names. When she found this same company was going to promote a local festival, she went to the committee and told them she would do it "for free" for the exposure. And she got a "dot com" site for them that later on became so valuable that other places wanted to buy it. That started her on her own business so she could stay home with her children. She took on other clients and a number of other non-profits, some of which she does for free. It took a few years to build her company, but it is now very successful.

Her present husband Mike, who was a Captain in the Air Force and is now retired, is using some of his skills to volunteer with the police department in our city as the Coordinator for the Volunteer Police Force, and Lin is also a volunteer there to help with traffic and parking during some of the busy times at the summer Festivals.

Love Fashion?

Joyce, a smart-looking woman of almost 60 today, first worked at AT&T and developed her telephone and speaking skills there. Then she decided to be a Nurse and studied that. An attractive lady, she did some modeling and finally some narrating of fashion shows and at that point decided to try to do videos of these shows. By then she was over 50 years old. She took classes at Community Television in her city and started her own TV program about fashion and the events going on for many non-profits. Gradually they began asking her to put on some events and fashion shows of her own. She found local models, makeup people and hair stylists and found the stores who would like to show their fashions and would hire her to do this. It grew into a part time job for pay. This evolved into teaching some classes on Personal Development, especially for teens. Today she is very successful in her own business.

Help Other Seniors

Two other women found a need and decided to open their own business. One of these is Barbara, a pretty blonde of 55, who helps Seniors find places to go when they leave their own homes to go to Retirement Living, Assisted Living or Convalescent Care, three different types of places. She named the business "Ask Barbara" and found another Barbara in an adjacent county to do the same type of consulting there so they could sometimes work together.

These businesses are familiar with all the possibilities and help people to determine which type of place will be best for them. Barbara says that the level of care in each place is most important; talking to the family is also important and finding out who makes the decisions for the person. Also she asks how close to family should the person be? What are the care givers at the facilities like (men or women, young or old)? Are there other couples there, if they are a couple? What activities are available? She also stresses that transportation and food choices are all important. Then will the family be able to join in at important times? All these questions will be answered for each place considered so that the outcome is a happy one for the Senior and for the family.

Another woman with her own business, Teresa, a short, energetic woman with springy curly hair about 55 years old, will help people with an entire move for a Senior, such as what to take and where to put everything in their new place. She calls it "A Move made Simple". Her services are useful for a move to a smaller home or a mobile one in a park, as well as to those above. She will also help with small things such as mail change, floor plans to scale to fit everything in the new place, find a mover and unpack everything personally. She has a housecleaning service as well to help people get their old place ready for sale or rent. Finally she gives help to people to get ready to move, by helping them decide what to get rid of by going through drawers and closets with them. She can also help in decisions about what to give to charity, family or the trash, the most difficult decisions of all!

Like to Bake?

Wearing a large white shirt (not the usual baker's hat) and sporting tiny pearl-drop earrings with her blonde casual hairdo, bangs and all, Catherine, 62, told me about her struggle to become a baker. Her two older brothers had become a doctor and a lawyer, and she, being the youngest, told her parents she wanted to become a baker. She says it must have shocked them enough that they thought it was as bad as opening a brothel by the way they reacted, because it was not what they had in mind for their daughter. So being a good girl, she went to college and majored in film. She floundered around after college with nothing in sight for her career and became an aerobics instructor for various spas. She also worked in Journalism for a while but became bored with that.

Then she started making these chocolate cookies that so many people had liked at her children's school and for several organizations to which she belonged. People kept telling her, she should sell them. So she did and then started expanding to cakes and other desserts to sell to people she knew. Then she realized that it was against the law to use your own kitchen to sell any food, so found there were several kitchens locally that were for rent that were approved by the Health Department to cook and sell your wares. She rented one and started her own business. She hired an accountant to keep the books and finally had the completely joyous experience of baking to her heart's content! Her cookies can be found in many local coffee shops in the city where she lives.

Caregiving for Others

Very attractive, sports-loving Mary, 65, wanted to supplement her income when she retired and since she had raised her own family and was now living alone, she took some training to become a Caregiver. She was assigned to care for two sisters who lived apart; each wanted to stay in their own homes and yet neither could drive to see the other. She takes them shopping and out to lunch so they can have some time with each other and does other light chores for each of them at their homes. She's close enough to their ages to become a real friend as well as their Caregiver. There are many local agencies in most places who hire people like Mary to care for others their own age but who are not as physically able as their Caregivers. It's a wonderful second career and one where one can earn some extra money as well.

Own a Motor Home?

Roland and his wife, a very attractive, vivacious couple of retirement age, own their motor home and loved to travel in it, especially to visit their children who live in various parts of the country but really don't have a guest room. Then they grew tired of moving around, so they found a job which they could do for part of the year to stay in one place and enjoy the area.

It all started when they visited Yosemite National Park in California and found that there were no spaces left in the campground for them to stay. They saw the HOST sign on one of the spaces and inquired about that job. They discovered that there was an opening for a host who could stay there in a self-contained unit, which they had, so they interviewed for the job. When the interviewer heard that Roland had climbed Half Dome and that they had been there before, a number of times, they were hired for the next three months. It's a Volunteer job, but you get to stay in most wonderful places for free for several months!

In each job they act as greeters and have to check several times a day to make sure that new people had any questions answered or problems solved and then to remind them of the day they had to leave. Of course many of the campers would say, "Already?"

Most of the time there are two Hosts, so that they work on alternate days, three days one week and four the next. They enjoyed their time in their first job so much that they looked into other parks and found two State Beaches on the California Coast that needed hosts, so they stayed a while in each. That's where I met them. They were headed next to Oregon and then later would stay with one of their grown children...in their mobile home of course. They ended up selling the house where they had lived and made moving around their way of life.

Becoming Parents Again

There are a number of people in their retirement who become parents again for various reasons. It could be a sad case of drugs or alcoholism or just that the parents both need to work and can't afford sitters all day. Or their son or daughter might be a single parent and they are helping with that difficulty. True, there are a number of pre-schools now for the young ones, but they cost money and it can be less expensive for a relative to take the job since they usually love doing it. You won't be alone if this becomes a job for you for a while. Even when the youngsters go to school, transportation is often needed, and you can help there. When it's part of your family, you would probably enjoy it as well.

Mechanic to Jewelry Making

Hugh was a mechanic most of his life and loved working with his hands. He worked on cars, trucks and even busses. When he moved to Arizona to retire, he was excited about the geology of the area and spent time looking for stones. Polishing them led to making jewelry with them and today he is selling many of his pieces and not only enjoying doing it but, in his retirement, starting a whole new business.

Hair Stylist to Own Shop

With beautiful, long, black, curly hair, Karen, not quite 50 yet, says she didn't do well in high school and wanted to get out as fast as possible so she found she could earn 10 extra units by signing up for an ROP program (experience in the real world). She was assigned to help in a Beauty Shop and found she was very good at this, so upon graduation she assisted the owner of a shop for a year, doing the shampoos and other "grunt" work. She stayed for three more years there and started doing her own clients, usually walk-ins, until she got a job working in another shop for several more years. Her next shop was working with 20 other hair stylists and learning a great deal from all of them. It finally closed, so she and four of the others decided to open a co-op, bringing their own clients and dividing the work around the shop. When two of them, a husband and wife, decided to open their own shop nearer to where they lived and another became pregnant and didn't want to work for a while, they all decided to let Karen and one other woman go it together.

At this point, because the shop was on the second floor with no elevator, they were not very visible and couldn't see any hope for new clients or people passing by. So Karen started to look around for another location. She found one in a better place and her father decided to back her at the beginning to make the move, which she said she couldn't have done otherwise. He felt that she had proved her ability, working so hard and now was close to fifty years old. He told her that this was part of her inheritance so she'd better make it work. The other woman wanted to go with her but wanted to just handle selling the products in the salon and earn her station that way. The Salon would belong to Karen.

She redecorated the place beautifully, using all the old equipment from the other location, but coloring the walls in bright colors giving the place a very modern look. She had no trouble attracting other stylists she had worked with to rent stations there, and today they all seem to be very happy. There is also more foot traffic there so they pick up more clients all the time. Now she has a good investment, for the day when she gets tired of standing so long. Karen will someday be able to sit down and run the shop, giving her a good income in her second fifty years.

Teacher to Owner of Management Company

A descendent of Norwegian parents, blonde, blue-eyed Jeanne studied in college to be a teacher since that was one field that she could get a scholarship from to attend college. Actually, she didn't want to be a teacher but she did follow the career for a number of years, to earn money when she first married. At 50 however, she got a divorce and found herself with three children and wanting a change in her life. She had taken a few Real Estate classes and decided to go for a Broker's license which she attained. She looked around for a need in her community and was asked by a few friends to manage their rentals. She started out with 10, with people she knew and then decided to take an early retirement from teaching and use the money to open her own office in property management. Today she has three employees and manages 150 properties, everything from cabins in the woods and condos to large houses. Recently, one of her daughters started working for her and is now working on her Brokers license so that in a few years, when Jeanne would like to retire to travel more with her new husband, she can take over the business.

CHAPTER 8
RETIRED MILITARY

There are so many ideas for Retired Military if you are too young to retire from the world!

Working at a University

After retiring from the Army, Gordon became the Operations Manager at a University to hire part-time people for odd jobs around the buildings and grounds. He has hired many people over 50 since he feels they bring many advantages to these jobs. They have skills acquired throughout their lives in the military or other jobs, and these can often be very useful to the University. He will even hire some people on a temporary basis to get something painted or welded when they couldn't hire someone full-time to do this. If they have been military, they will feel comfortable with him as the "boss".

Help Others To Do What You Have Done

Retired as a Captain in the Air Force, Michael and his family moved around a great deal after his marriage while he was flying. He had also moved around as a child, being in a military family growing up. He and his wife realized what a job it was each time to go to another location. They finally settled in the Santa Cruz area to be near his wife's father who was failing rapidly. They found an Assisted Living place for him and picked out the furniture and things he wanted most to take with him. It was then that they realized how difficult it was for older people to choose things to use in a smaller place when they needed to go. So they took some training, went to the Small Business Administration to get help getting a license and started their own business called "Perfect Changes" where they help elderly people with that kind of a move. Many of the local retirement homes suggest their company to incoming clients, and they found much satisfaction in helping these people make decisions about what to take, and what to leave, sell or give away to a non-profit. They later found another couple to go in with them and contracted with a moving company to move the heavy furniture. They, however, choose and move the smaller things themselves and help decide where things could go in the new location. Their experience in so many moves helps them in these decisions. It is a perfect part-time job for them.

Become a Master Gardener

Mary was an Army Nurse and ended her career in Washington, DC at the Pentagon in the under-secretary office doing medical work. Her children grew up there and still visit back and forth, even after she came West when she retired. She started jewelry-making to earn a little extra income, until her hands gave her some problems and she couldn't continue. She had always loved gardening, even in Washington, but in California she found the Master Gardening classes and got certified as a Master Gardener. She found them on line and learned they were constantly training people.

At present, Mary is working hard in the local Homeless

Garden and is on their Board of Directors. This is a community garden, not just for homeless, but for anyone who wants to work there. They sell their produce and have a lunch each week with the produce and sell things in their store. There are three full-time staff there and three part-time in their store. They also provide produce to several other local stores. About one-third of the people who volunteer there and learn, end up with paying job. They have a hot-line to answer questions about anything in your garden and a web site available to people. Mary has a lovely garden in her own back yard with many, many succulents and she spends some spare time as a Docent at a local State Park right on the beach a few blocks from where she lives. They too have a garden, so she can use her acquired expertise to help there too.

CHAPTER 9
HOW ABOUT ART?

Art has been an interest for many people but few seem able to make a living from it without teaching on the side. If you have another income from your retirement, it might be a good time to develop skills that may have been put aside earlier in your life as "not a very practical career." If so, now might be the time to get out that paint brush, not just for re-doing the bedroom walls, but to try something new.

From PE Teacher to Art

When I met Annie, 62, she was wearing a colorful red and green shirt with a scoop neckline following the curve of her long brown hair upon her shoulders. She told me that she had lived in a city with many museums, so she grew up loving to go to them and seeing the Art. In 5th grade she was chosen to do a mural in her classroom during a short vacation and when the teacher and students came back they were very surprised! The teacher asked the class "Has anyone ever seen a purple cow?" They all laughed and shook their heads "No." Annie was so angry and embarrassed that she decided then and there to never do anything artistic again! Instead, after she was told that girls didn't become Doctors or Engineers which had been her first choices, she decided to become a PE teacher. She loved sports and the out-of-doors, so this was an obvious career. She especially loved Gymnastics since she could design the costumes and that was where she felt her creative juices come to life.

Later, after getting divorced, she ran a ski shop until she met her second husband who wanted to move to California. There she started a woman's boutique shop and because she was the owner, she could design the windows. She loved that so much that it interfered with her sales because she was always thinking of her next window. Finally they moved to be near the ocean which she loved and as she was surfing she had a terrible accident with a wave that dropped her on her head. Her right arm was also badly hurt. So at 57 years old, she felt that her life was over when a friend suggested she go to a class about clay modeling. This might help her arm and shoulder to exercise them. She did this until a kiln blew up in her face! Finally her right arm and shoulder had healed, so she decided to try painting which turned out to be a life saver for her. She took some classes and eventually had her own show of all her paintings and started to sell some of them. She even influenced her 92-year old mother to start painting.

When she made a visit to Mexico and saw all the handicrafts and art made there, she became inspired to buy some and returned to California to show her fellow artists. Many of them wanted to buy what she had brought back, so this inspired her to start a whole new business, going down there to buy and return back to sell. This way she could help some of these people and pay for her trips at the same time.

Salesman to Artist

Mel, 68, looked like he had just come off the beach with his permanent tan and hooded, smiling eyes. He told me that he had worked for an International Wine company in the East for years and ended up selling a non-alcoholic wine. Then when he retired, he felt like true retirement was a death sentence, so he had to think of something to do. He needed some reason to get out of bed each morning. Tennis and golf were not enough.

He had traveled to France in his job and one day there saw a man pulling off fliers from a pole, which were all over the place, and so thick because people would put one flier on top of another. So when he scraped them off himself, he found there were many layers with all these beautiful colors on the edges. Mel became inspired to make collages with these papers. This was his inspiration, so he followed with other collages that used more "found" objects and put them together in frames. This, he decided, would be what he would do in retirement. He collected all kinds of things to put into his collages and soon found that people were interested in them and wanted to buy them. So there he was, in a new business with something that he loved doing. He met many people who were excited with what he was doing, so he helped them get started too. He doesn't feel the competition they might bring. Today, he feels that if he can inspire someone else to do something similar, he's happy!

Psychology & Anthropology to Paper Folding

Hiding behind her glasses which shaded her eyes a little, soft-speaking Gloria, now 75, wanted to be an artist when she was a little girl. She looked at paintings, mostly in oil, and sculpture and sighed and wondered how people could make these things look so real! However, she needed a more practical choice in college, so majored in Psychology and Anthropology and worked at a mundane job to help put her husband through college. After being a housewife and mother for a number of years, at age 40 she decided to fulfill her dreams of becoming an artist. So she applied to several Art schools, but of course she didn't have anything to show them to get in (which they required) so she was rejected. Then she decided to enroll in the Home Economics program where she could take some art classes as electives. While there she started to do something with cloth, like quilting but only single scenes that she could frame. She won first place in a contest with her first one, so she continued doing that, working on cloth. She learned silk screening and combined that with her stitching and later started including plastic sheets. Some of these looked like collages, but she said they were screen prints with the plastic sheets as part of the pieces. She won many prizes along the way for her innovative work.

Then the computer came along and she started incorporating that into her work. She printed on linen, made a full-sized man out of computer chips and then moved on to paper folding. She went to New York City to look for some posters from a local furniture store and took along a few of her paper designs. Showing them to a woman at one of the local boutiques, the woman said that she'd take both of them to sell and anything else she might have. This led to other galleries in New York wanting her unusual works.

After taking some more classes, Gloria started to make her own paper and other people started to notice her work with paper folding. Gloria admitted that she never really learned to paint, but her artistic self came through with all kinds of other creative ideas. She realized that if she had started painting, she'd be competing with very well-trained and fabulous artists who'd been doing that for years, but by being innovative, she was a leader in this field. At the time, she had no competition in paper folding and knew that she would be noticed. And she was!

Styrofoam

With his very expressive face and eyes moving all over the place, David, 68, talked to me about his latest passion. He had decided late in his life, to use Styrofoam to make his sculptures, then cover them with concrete. The foam is not biodegradable and just sits there in a land fill, so he has found a use for it. He's now making fountains for backyards and other sculptures that are very attractive outdoors. Most of them are quite large because he can pile one upon another to make a tall sculpture. They are not too expensive to make since he finds the Styrofoam everywhere, often discarded from boxes of equipment. He also likes to paint on stone, paintings that also could be used in a garden.

Apparently David was always doing large art because his acrylic paintings are also huge, huge birds in flight with large wing spans. He loves animals and tended to paint these, like his beautiful painting of Japanese Koi fish, also a huge painting. So now he's taking orders for the Styrofoam creations and in his retirement has a very unusual hobby that's good for the environment, and we all want to help with that!

Wood to Sand

Then there's Kirk, 66, a tall slender Scandinavian-type who

was a wood carver for many years and did ice sculpture as well for local parties. Now in the second half of his life, he's discovered sand sculpture. With his partner Rusty, he taught a group of Docents at a California State Park Beach how to make large sand sculptures. I was one of them and carried my knowledge on to my family reunion on the beach. We learned that the key for the sculptures is to use plenty of water. Pack it down and down again. Then sculpt. We made a beautiful one that was admired by all who passed by.

Kirk went on to enter sand sculpture contests throughout the world and eventually the Travel Channel sponsored him and his crew to make a television series, showing them putting together sculptures for various commercial organizations and parties. This lasted almost half a year. Now he and his group are in great demand for parties put on by business and family groups all over the world. Yes, they can make them even along rivers in Germany or they can bring in sand from elsewhere to make the sculptures at a museum. Sand sculptures are a great group activity because they are fun to help make and beautiful to look at!

Donate Wooden Toys

"If you can help others when you retire, it's probably the greatest thing you can do." That's what Al says. At 89 he has a modern butch haircut on his white hair and there's an excitement in his voice as he talks about what he is doing in his retirement. He makes toys out of wood in his garage and donates them to a non-profit agency to give them away to needy children. He is in a club that meets for lunch monthly to compare notes and show each other some of the latest toys they have made.

Early in his life he was a Manufacturer's Sales Representative, but started getting some of his wood-working equipment and making the toys when his first grandchild came along. He has a large poster card showing how to make a toy with the sizes and shapes of all the parts, to help someone new to the field make a wooden grasshopper. He has made all kinds of toys, from the usual cars, trains and planes to a tall push-cart that makes noise from things inside when the child pushes it as he/she walks. He also has a small basketball hoop, with a spoon holding the ball that can get flipped into the hoop. He has so many clever ideas, some of which came from a magazine about this. I was very impressed with the number of toys that he has made. He's so excited and enthusiastic about doing this. And the children who get them, I'm sure, are very happy and grateful.

Try Curating

With horned-rim glasses, Judy, 57, looked at me with a big smile showing off her beautiful white teeth. Her soft, sweet voice told about how she had become a sculptor but later moved into printmaking, glass and acoustic, willing to try all the different media. No wonder she was asked to became a curator at a local museum, since she knew and had worked with various media. A curator puts the exhibits together, decides where each piece will hang or be placed. Curating requires many hours of helping the artists to choose what works to show and hanging them so they can best be seen in the gallery. This one had many small rooms because it was originally a private home. The gallery itself has become a medium of its own.

Her friend Mary, 62, a white-haired short-built lady, also

became a curator with Judy on a local exhibit featuring "Eight Artists Over Eighty in '08". She is also a printmaker and painter. Together the two women also created a beautiful 84-page catalogue of the show, with images of much of the art work. Although entrance to the show was free, a donation was asked, and the museum did charge extra for the catalogue, pleasing the two creative women who designed it.

The following eight artists were in this exhibit. Most of them learned art early in their lives, however most of them changed from one type to art to another in their retirement. Some came from teaching and are now doing their own art. Also, some started writing or doing some other type of artistic expression. Here they are:

From House Painting

Wearing an open-front zippered gray sweatshirt, Al, now 82, squinted his eyes as he talked about only having an 8th-grade education since both his parents died and he was on his own at the age of 14. So he apprenticed with a house painter, learned to make his own paint and how to color it and learned much about the technology of paint. At 18 he joined the Army Air Corps and traveled a good deal, got married at 20 and moved to Alaska. Leaving his wife and new baby, he promised to send for them as soon as he could make a living. His wife's father thought he was running away from her. Actually, he did regularly send her money during that time and finally sent for her to join him. He painted a church in Sitka, built his own boat and fished for a living. There he also learned woodcarving and became interested in that, so used his GI Bill to move down and attend college in Los Angeles to study art. There he taught

Ceramics at the University until he retired to a house he had built in the state of Washington overlooking the harbor. Physically built it himself.

This is when he got into oil painting and modeling with clay. The latter was most interesting to him and from there he started casting in bronze. However, he says, this took up too much room, so he decided to try wood-block painting. He was happy with this, because then he could get rid of all the other equipment that was taking up room in his home.

Dresses to Figurines

I caught Helen, 74, in her workshop working on putting faces on elongated pots. Wearing a royal blue shirt complementing her short grayish hair, she told me she was a dress designer at the beginning of her career. Then when she had three children, she switched to handicrafts. She and her husband owned a Summer Camp and there was a college nearby where she could take some Art classes. The only one where she could "come and go" was a class in Ceramics. So she decided to take that.

Each year when they went to their camp, she took another class and decided that she really liked it and was very good at it. She sold one of her little figures of a lady with a cute hat to a commercial company and they put it on Ebay, manufactured it commercially and got $250 for each one! They made a quarter of a million dollars for this. Her work is very whimsical and fun to look at, because they are not just jars or cups but all have a face on them, or are a twist to what you would think they should be. She's become very successful.

After Teaching

Don, age 68, sporting a mustache to go with his dark gray hair, told me that art had been all around him growing up and he had gone to museums often in his early life. He traveled around a good deal from the East to Colorado and finally to California, always very interested in art. But to make a living out of it, he decided to study Commercial Art and then finally Fine Art. Never really planning to become a teacher, he was offered a job teaching at a University and spent most of his life doing that, never finding time to make art himself. He was too busy teaching others. Now that he is retired from teaching, he finds jobs in painting a few portraits and making prints from his art. He says that he has no formula, but just starts painting and it comes alive as he goes. Not sure that will work for me, but it seems to work for him, and maybe you!

Doodles Lead On

Plump, bald with a grey mustache, 73-year-old Manny told me he majored in Education so that he could make a living teaching but ended up working in factories and restaurants to earn enough for his family. He liked to doodle with a pencil and someone who saw that told him to try Art as a career because he was very good and seemed to have some natural talent. Out of the Army, he took some courses and started to draw faces which seemed to be very popular. But he never could make a living at it. So in his retirement he rented a warehouse and has a huge gallery today with his works on display. He also has a huge printing press to make prints. Today he is able to sell many of them and he is very happy.

A Life of Different Art

A very sweet lady, over 80, Marta, was one of the lucky ones who had a husband with a good job, so she has been able to enjoy doing her Art without having to sell it. Her husband worked in the business office at a University so she was able to pursue her Art much of her life. When she was younger she did murals and a beautiful diorama for a Museum of Modern Art. She had more offers to do murals but turned them down, she says, because they took too much climbing. Then she really enjoyed Life Drawing classes at the University using real models, but lately she does PleinAir painting which is painting scenes outdoors usually with other artists. She's also interested in making collages and paper folding. Today, she seems to sell quite a few of her works, but says she wouldn't try to make a living out of that. In her and her husband's retirement, she just wants to enjoy doing it.

Woodcuts

A gentleman named Carol, in his 70's with white hair and a small pony tail, had a father who taught painting and did Medical Illustrations, so he was able to study Art at an early age from his father. He thinks of himself as a printer, today doing woodcuts of pine and plywood, cutting the designs with a knife and then printing them in different colors on paper. Sometimes the colors run through to the other side making interesting patterns on both sides of the paper. To do this he is using solvents, and mineral spirits to dissolve the inks. It's something different and although he does some teaching and several workshops, he enjoys just making the art.

Trumpeting to Glass

White-haired and dressed warmly in a blue open collar shirt over a magenta one when I interviewed her, Betty told me that she had studied music and played the trumpet for years, until she got interested in Sculpture. So she learned welding, which was very difficult, and used sheet metal and bronze for her sculptures. She did this for years along with teaching the craft. Later she enjoyed working with glass and making mosaics out of old pottery. I saw some of her beautiful works, one of mosaics on a metal bowl and also many glass objects. However, she says today she is ready to sit down more at her age of 80 and has taken up writing. The other is too physical!

Art to Poetry

Doug taught Painting and Design, as well as Art History at a University and got interested in computer-generated Art. However, now in his retirement he is enjoying writing Poetry. He does Free Verse and has self-published several books of his works.

He travels to Mexico quite frequently and still does some art there, where he takes photos and puts them into Open Boxes as frames, with other objects in a sort of collage. They are very different from anything else I have seen. Again, here is someone who is artistic and can move from one medium to another, art to poetry.

CHAPTER 10
MUSICIANS NEEDED

They say that students who study music do better in school, particularly in Math, so this is a good time for you to teach whatever aspect of music you have accomplished. It's really an international language. There's sometimes even a local group you might join to hone your skills and just enjoy!

Pharmacy to Piano Lessons

Joni, a pretty, petite silver-haired lady with a personality that belies her 70 years, studied music in college at a University and then went to Drake to study piano. She was headed for a concert career, but since money was an object, she needed to get a job. Since she was very attractive, with a vivacious way of speaking, she easily became a stewardess with an airline and ultimately ran a style show for them. Then she met her husband who was a Pharmacist and decided to help him with his business. She ran the front end of the Pharmacy for about twenty years, until a huge drug store moved in nearby and put them out of business! Since they had at least saved some money, they decided to take the time to travel for awhile, and loved that. However, a few years later, sadly, her husband died so she had to decide what to do next. Never one to be fazed, she opened a Consignment Shop to use the skills she had running a business.

Today, she has gone back to her music, playing organ at her church and playing piano at parties for background music. She also did two-piano duets at various places with a partner until the other woman passed away. Then trying to keep doing what she loved which was music, she checked with other music teachers to find the latest books they used in teaching, since she had been out of doing that for many years. Now she is teaching young people and especially loves teaching duets, which she does locally to a brother and sister. She discovered that playing the piano is usually a skill one never forgets. However, she is still taking organ lessons from a local woman and jazz lessons at a Community College to improve her skills. Joni never gives up and this keeps her busy and happy.

Senior Musical Shows

A very sweet and pretty lady, Wanda, 65, worked in the Housing Department at a University for years, but she had always loved to dance. So when at 62 years of age, she heard about a local group at a Senior Center that put on monthly musicals and needed some dancers, she turned up on Thursday morning and they put her right away into the chorus. Then when they practiced with the singers the following week she asked if they thought that maybe she could sing in the chorus as well, so they let her do that also. She was having such a great time, so when they asked her to sing in a trio for the next show, she did it. In the next show after that they put her into singing a duet, and a few shows later she was doing a solo! She never thought she could ever do that when she started, but they were cute songs and she loved doing it.

Before she knew it, she was assisting the director of one of the shows and she really enjoyed that. One thing led to another. You guessed it! She finally directed her own show. Now she admits that directing has become her favorite thing to do. At the beginning if anyone had told her she would be directing shows, she would have thought they were crazy!

More Musicals

Lois, 67, who seems very quiet until you get to know her, worked for years at Wrigleys and retired with a pension enabling her to do what she wanted in retirement. She had always sung in her Church choirs and elsewhere, so when she heard about the Senior Center doing a show, she decided to try out. "Try out? They would take anyone who came", she said, but having a beautiful voice, it made it easy for them to assign her to some solos. Later they asked her to assist the director and that led eventually to directing her own show. Since the various directors there get a chance to direct one show only once a year, she's always thinking of ideas for a new show. It's something to keep her mind busy and to think about, after caring for an ill husband. Now that he has passed away, she's happy to be doing something that brings so much happiness to others.

Tall, graceful Alice at a young 59, is the choreographer for this group. She had always loved dance and movement and coming to the Choraliers she had a chance to do that. She too, although she had never studied to become a Choreographer, sort of fell into it when the person doing it became ill. She found that she could work with other seniors giving them simple dance steps to fit with different kinds of music. It was a challenge but she loved it. Now she gets the music for each show months ahead and works out the steps just from her past experience. Her dancers are all volunteers for each show and have to practice once a week for the two months before each show, but they all love dancing and her, so it's no work at all! And great exercise!

Music and Theatre

Arresting eyes and beautiful white teeth stand out on Lynn's face as she excitedly talks about "StAGEbridge", the new performing arts classes designed especially for lifelong learners 50 and up. Yes, the "AGE" in the middle of the word is meant to be there in capital letters. Lynn, now 65, was a dancer on Broadway for many years and coming to a resort town in California, she was looking for something to do in her retirement, so she joined up with a local Community College to present a week of classes in the summer for older Actors, Singers and Dancers. It was based on an idea that has worked in Oakland, CA for several years, and now it's working elsewhere. There are professional teachers for the classes and the purpose is to have fun and join with others locally in the arts. Perhaps you could start one in your community.

CHAPTER 11
PHOTOGRAPHY

Most of us have taken pictures in our lives whether with a Brownie Camera or the latest hand-held phone or tablet. It's great as a hobby, but maybe it could be more than that in your case.

Nursing to Photography

Two nurses, a man and women, met at their church and started talking and discovered they had much in common. Patrick, 64, a jovial, heavy-set gentleman, had Military Training in nursing, so later he worked for many years for a company that involved nursing. Then he decided that it was time to retire so he started doing some photography for their church. At that point he met Kathie, a sweet gentle lady of 62, who had also been a nurse but was in a wheelchair and very ill; in fact she had really practically been at death's door for a long time. However, she said when she saw his smile and discovered that he was a photographer, she was very excited. She had been taking pictures all of her life and really enjoyed doing it. She also knew that she could no longer be a nurse. So they started taking short trips together. Point Lobos in Northern California was the first. Since then, they've been there more than 14 times with always something to see in the water or near the edge of the ocean.

They started doing this together while she was in a wheelchair, then a walker and then graduating to just a cane, so this really did help in her rehabilitation. Now they can go anywhere because she can walk on her own. They loved shooting animals, so they invested in better lenses and cameras that could shoot multiple times as the animals moved. Now they have moved into wedding photography, a school yearbook and, of course, still for their church occasions.

They are also interested in Macro photography, looking at something in an extreme close-up so people can try to figure out what it is. They showed me still pictures of a campfire close-up, rocks that have faces, and trees that look like something else close up. They also enjoy taking pictures of their reflections in a mud puddle. This is a very exciting experience!

One of Patrick's photos will appear in the Library of Congress' coffee table book of the year and one of Kathie's will be in another book. They realize that now they can consider themselves professional and look forward to many happy years working together.

Dance to Photography

With attractive brown eyes and hair, 58-year-old Serafina started learning about creative dance and art therapy in college and then her school went bankrupt before she could finish. She wanted to do something in the arts but something that also could fulfill her love for working with people. She was trying to think about what to do when her grandfather died and left her some of his photography equipment, and she decided to try that out. At first she was just filming objects until someone asked her to do a wedding. That was good training because she found she enjoyed working with these people to do this but also found that she needed two cameras and equipment. So she got the equipment and she did more weddings. From there she went into doing portraits, working to introduce some fantasy into her pictures. She eventually started to take some courses with Professional Photographers of America, and got a Masters Degree.

Serafina realized that she needed to work in a studio so she decided to build one. She then started collecting costumes and props that would help with some of the portraits. She says that she tries to capture the personality of each of her subjects. She starts with a little makeup, then gives them some costumes and after a few hours she finds that their true personality comes out. She thinks of photography as an art. So she tries out many different techniques, such as varying the paper on which she prints her photos. She also uses the computer to make changes in her photographs. She says that Photography has to be a business because it costs money for equipment and one needs to market their talents to get started. Recently she also started teaching at a Community College and really enjoys that.

Video to Photos

After being a stewardess before marriage, Judy became a homemaker and wife for a number of years. She went back to college at the age of 35, majoring in Drama and Speech and got the chance to interview several of the teachers there for a local television station. She did interviews for two years while at the college, then continued working for the television station for another two years.

Actually all of her life she had taken photos of her family and had also used an 8mm film camera and an audio tape recorder to tape conversations of them at the dinner table and other places. Finally she decided to copy all of that film onto a video camera, adding the audio to make 4 six-hour videos that she could present to them at Christmas.   But she still hadn't thought of this as a career to earn a living. So to earn something, she opened a store in her town featuring local crafts and put her photographs up on the walls. They started to sell.

Judy also contacted artists from all over the county to put their art in her store and started to sell space to them and, of course, she sold their art since she lived in a very busy tourist area near the ocean in California. Then, after three successful years, the city decided that a parking lot would have to go in there for an Aquarium that needed it. So that ended her store! Smiling, she told me that she believed (as I do actually) that if one door closes in life, another will open! A very up-beat lady!

Knowing she was available, the Art and Wine Festival of her city asked her to be the official photographer for the Festival, and from that she sold many of her photographs and started her on her way to being considered a Professional Photographer! One of the local hotels bought two of her photos to be used in the lobby of the hotel. Two of her photographs of Yosemite were sold to an Embassy in Washington, D.C. and two to an aviation company. She also sold a number of note cards with her photos on them. Today, at the age of 60, this plucky, very attractive lady is into using her computer, after taking a few classes locally about how to use it with her pictures. With that knowledge she started restoring some old photos and has made another business out of that. There's another idea for you photographers!

Electronics

I enjoyed interviewing tall, slender, white-haired, 70-year-old, Larry who has an expressive face. His eyebrows raised as he talked, making creases in his wide forehead. His father had a television and radio repair shop so he grew up learning a bit about some of the technical aspects of this. He left high school to join the Army and got into Radar school there and ended up on a mountain top in Alaska working with missiles. From there he went to Texas to work in electronics systems and so on, moving up in the field, doing sales, becoming a Manager in various companies, but working seven days a week. So at one point in 2002, he took his stock and left and now considers himself retired. But along the way, he was always interested in photography. He learned this by just trying things, experimenting and seeing what turns out. Since he never took a class in this, it was just instinctive. Larry has several cameras depending upon the job and a huge printer that will print a six foot picture, because he likes to shoot pictures that will go on walls in restaurants and businesses. He still considers it a hobby and refuses to take pay for his work. Then, he says, he'd still be working and he doesn't want to do that!

Advertising to Photos & Writing

I met pretty, curly-red-haired Leah at a skating rink during the US Figure Skating Championships. She was taking pictures of the skaters at rink side. We talked and I discovered that she worked for the Yellow Pages selling advertising and hoped to retire in the next year when she would become 50. She was the first person I met who was excited and happy to be turning 50! She hopes to retire in Grand Junction, Colorado with the fresh air and freedom to do what she wants.

She had planned this retirement at 50 for years, working for 30 years and saving her money. She and her husband are going to relocate, where she will work with Alzheimer's patients and other non profits and continue with her photography following the figure skaters around the world. She skated herself until she was 41. Now she is going to do the advertising for a new rink in this town and continue with her photography since she is so well known among the skaters. That will enable her to continue her travel all over the world, so she is very excited about that.

She knew what she wanted to do and that was to continue with her photography. I now see her name with her photos in some of the Figure Skating magazines and she has done a number of covers for them. She also sets up interviews with the skaters and takes photos of them in various costumes. She then sells her pictures to them. She has also sold some of her photos to books who want pictures of the champions.

So if you have a love of a sport or something else, taking pictures of it, still or video, can lead to a second career for pay or just for fun!

CHAPTER 12
TELEVISION AND FILM

This, of course, was my field and here am I in a new field, writing a book! There is always something interesting around the corner, if you just look. Television and Film are really the same fields, just a different method of recording. The film is developed and is a permanent recording, while the television production is usually on a chip or tape which can be reused, so is more practical especially in learning.

While I was teaching in college, a student came into the television studio where my class was being held and said "I thought I was taking a Film Class, not TV! I'm going to a Film School!" And he turned around and left. I heard that he went to LA to a film school and later I received a letter from him, apologizing and telling me that I was right, they were starting him out using a video camera. Of course. Many of the same techniques are used and it's less expensive than film on which to learn, especially with the advent of digital recording.

TV Ideas

When I met Harriet, 78, with short gray hair, no makeup, she told me that she had been a teacher for many years and later was counseling students about drug, alcohol and cigarette smoking. With a number of Masters Degrees, she became an Omsbudsman for a company to help their

Executives who had substance abuse problems. Then she had an idea for a TV show called "Information Society" which she couldn't sell, and that's when she found out that television is a business and you need to find sponsors. So she created another show called "Word of the Day", a little filler between shows which was picked up by one station back East and they paid her. Finally she produced a "Real Estate Show" which appeared at a station in the area where she retired. She continues to do this today.

Children's News Program

I also found out how difficult it was to break into National Television with a new idea, even after having worked in the industry. After I left the CBS affiliate in Sacramento, California with my experience as a News Anchor and Interviewer, I decided to create a Children's News Program. I knew a very talented Puppeteer and decided to use a huge globe background with my oldest daughter as the commentator and three puppets as the reporters. Another local TV channel in my city agreed to do a pilot. I wrote the news for that day, had Sheldon the Swordfish puppet swim to the State of Florida (using special effects) which showed on the globe, and he reported while peeking out from the water. Then Celia the Bird flew to a Kentucky coal mine where there was an explosion and that city showed up on the map. Next was Horace the horse who did the sports and could run to the area shown to talk about some horse races in Idaho. So I had put in some geography as well as reporting news that would be important to children.

The station loved the show and sent me down to LA to show it to the NBC network, where the Producer I met loved the show also. However, the bosses in the Children's department rejected the show because a news show cannot be rerun in the summer and any children's programs they broadcasted at the time, had to have reruns to make them financially viable.

Senior Programming

The next program I created was called (as the name of this book) "Your Second Fifty Years." I knew a number of people who were doing interesting things after the age of fifty so my old TV station agreed to produced several pilots of this show (with me working for nothing of course). We tried to find sponsors but they all declared that they didn't want to sponsor anything for people over 50 because they "probably didn't buy anything." Their target market at that time was in the ages 20s and 30s to people starting their own homes and who needed to purchase everything. So I started to write this book at that time in 1966, but never finished it. Years later I had the opportunity to develop this show for the local cable channel and have now produced over 500 shows. I pulled out that old manuscript and have added many of those interviews to hopefully inspire others to make their second 50 years as productive as possible. This is what I am doing in my second 50 years!

Hospital Operations

How about selling your skills to a different place? A student in one of my Television classes found there were no jobs locally in broadcasting when he graduated and since he didn't want to leave the area where he lived, he had to create his own job. He went to one of the local hospitals and talked them into buying the equipment and then he would prepare a video for the patients, to show them what their operation would be like, before and after, what doctors and nurses would be helping and so on. He had thought about what he wanted to do and where he wanted to be, and then created the perfect job for himself, even convincing someone else to hire him to do this.

Obituaries

I noticed in our newspaper an ad for doing a Television Obituary of your loved one. However, I have been doing Video Memories for many years. I interview the loved one and then we talk, while looking at many of the pictures in their scrapbook or on the wall in their home, keeping the camera on the picture. This makes them less nervous than keeping them on camera and I can edit and insert the pictures later. It's important to market this service to their grown children, before the older generation are no longer here! They'll be glad they did it.

Think of more ideas using your video camera!

CHAPTER 13
OTHER IDEAS

Here are some unique ideas from some people who don't fall into the other categories but are doing their own "thing" such as hobbies, special interests and helping others.

Animals

Her silver white hair, styled in a middle part and framing her face, lined with signs of life worth living, Shirley, now 75, studied Zoology and worked with animals for her career. Now that she's retired she is planning to go to another state as a Volunteer to help out in the Zoo there and start a program of Volunteers. She has been a Docent at a California State Beach where she lives and worked with them there for free as a volunteer, and realized the importance of volunteers to help out in other places. Many people love animals and would enjoy this activity when they retire. Is that for you?

Trains

What child can forget the trains around the Christmas tree? Many of them grew up to love trains later in life as well. Craig is one of these and today it's a huge hobby for him. Too young-looking to be retired, he is and at 78 is still physically fit and loves visiting ships and trains around the Western USA. He joined a group in San Jose that gets together to buy, trade and display their trains. They go into an empty store in a shopping center and bring a free attraction to the Mall. Promising to stay open certain hours, they allow the children (and some grownups too) to run the trains that they have set up in several areas. Their trains are reproductions of those in the 20s and 30s mostly. So it's a win/win proposition: They have fun setting up different configurations and the public can enjoy watching or participating. They also buy more cars or trains on the internet and trade with others to complete their set of various reproductions.

Ancestors

Very smart looking and dressing beautifully, Lois, 84, was a Resource Specialist for students with Learning Disabilities for much of her working life. When she retired, a friend got her interested in her ancestry and she was told to start with herself and go back from there, on-line at Ancestry.com. She followed her father's line first, then her mother's, and finally her husband's and put them all into spiral binders. She learned to scan some colored pictures and put these into the printed books for her families. Some of this was even of interest locally to the Historical Society for their use, as long as she did not include living persons without their permission. The information she finds can be helpful to others in her area since many might have some relationship to her family members. She finds it fun and very exciting to find people she never knew to be her relatives in the past, and learned much history in the doing. She feels that it's very rewarding.

Newcomers Club

At age 66, a slender brunette with flipped hair, Lynn's background is in counseling and she was a licensed Marriage and Family Therapist after her two boys were in school. She practiced for over 25 years and received excellent references from former patients, so was very busy working in that field. She lived in the inland valley in California, but she and her husband bought a condo on the beach for vacations, one that her children could use also. Then years later when they retired, they decided to move to the beach. She heard about the Newcomers Club there, so used to being involved with people in her work, she felt that she wanted to meet others in her new location. The purpose was to have fun and meet people. Many members stay a number of years in the club to help others who move there. This past year she became President of the Club with about 150 members. She loves it and finds that when you are new and living in a different area, it's very helpful and comforting to have immediate friends. Many cities and probably towns also have these groups.

Acting

Billie, 82, with her lovely British accent, which gives her a very cultured persona, beautifully groomed as well, told me she had wanted to go into Theatre before college but her parents frowned on her appearing on the "wicked stage." So she decided to go to Secretarial College instead. Forty years later she auditioned for a small part in the "Cherry Orchard" put on by a local group. To her surprise, they gave her the lead! That did it. She was smitten and it led to being in other plays at that small theatre. She was asked to read children's books on Saturday mornings on a local radio station, unpaid but she loved it. Then she organized radio dramas on this station with other actors she knew. She said that the only trouble with that was "when you finish on the radio there was no applause. You just went home!" So she turned to some paid jobs doing Shakespeare and loves working with other professionals where you "really learn a lot!" And you get lots of applause.

Tiny with an animated strong voice, 78-year-old Jean told me she studied Art History in college, visited Italy to see the great masters, and taught it at UCLA because she had always loved Museums. It wasn't until 35 years later that she took a small part in a local theatre play and decided that she liked it a great deal. Her experience as a teacher helped since she had developed a voice that could always be heard in the classroom. So she took a course on acting at a Community College and in her first role she appeared as a 80-year-old man in a Shakespeare play and working with professional actors. She's been acting ever since whenever they needed an older woman. She seems to find parts in theaters in two different cities, since she lives in between both, so is as busy as she wants to be and loves it.

Antiques

Karen, 55 a jolly smiling woman, always knitting when she can, making caps for new babies in the hospital, was a teacher of early grades K-3 in the MidWest and loved every minute of it. Then all the teachers over 50 got a Golden Handshake to retire early, so she took it and moved to California to be near more of her family. However, she discovered that California wouldn't give her a teaching credential even though she had taught Kindergarten for 30 years and had a Master's Degree. All she could do was substitute teach which gave her a little extra money.

Meanwhile, her grandmother had died and left her many very old pieces of furniture, dishes and knickknacks. She had always loved to visit antique stores and found a friend who owned one and who told Karen she could use a corner of her store to sell those things. There were four other women there who did the same thing and they all worked together to sell their antiques, taking a different day each week to work there.

This tied in with Karen's love of travel. She took a trip with her daughter to Paris and found many flea markets with interesting, cheap vintage objects. Filling her extra suitcase with these that she had bought, she was able to sell them all at a profit. This started her travel to other places in the world to pick up things that she felt would sell in the shop. She reads many books and magazines about antiques to help her in choosing the ones to buy, and of course is taking a chance on being able to sell them. So far, she has done well enough to finance her trips, so that has been a bonus for her retirement years.

Peace Corps

Most people think of the Peace Corps as populated with young people who join for experiences in the world and helping others. But Ellen and Terry think otherwise. Ellen retired after three terms as a County Supervisor and Terry as Executive Director of a Non-Profit for over 30 years. They both have law degrees and in their late 50s have joined the Peace Corps. It took a year of medical exams and interviews before they were accepted to go to Ethiopia to teach

English to teachers. They leave behind two married daughters, a son who graduated from college last year and another son finishing up college. So Ellen and Terry thought that this was the time to spend 27 months away before any grandchildren might be forthcoming. This had been their dream for many years. They will be training for several months in the country before they are assigned to teach and represent Americans in a positive way. We discussed the ins and outs of living conditions there but they seem to be ready for anything!

They will have to have a working knowledge of the language and are studying up on this. Since they will be living with a family, they expect that the language will come easily. They also hope to have the use of cell phones and hope they might have an internet connection there, unless they are located away from the major cities. Since they will be teaching English to teachers, they will probably be in a city. Sounds exciting and very brave!

Art & Poetry

Matt, now 51, looking like a "hippie" with his long, light brown hair and playful attitude, always enjoyed art and was encouraged by all his teachers. However to earn a living, he became a plasterer and tile layer for about 14 years. Then he met the love of his life, Karen who told him that his art was too important not to do full time. She arranged for him to go to various cities in California that had art festivals and he started painting "live" to music as people watched. He loved bright colors and put greens and blues in the backgrounds with oranges and reds in the fore with his bright acrylic paints.

One day a man came by and pulled out a set of 3D glasses and exclaimed to him "You did it!" "What?" Matt said. "You made 3D paintings that I have been trying to do for years. I paint with those glasses on, trying to do that, and you have done it already!" Matt was astounded when they looked at the many paintings he had with him at the festival and they all went into 3D with the glasses on. So he started to bring a pair to his showings and soon became known as the artist who paints in 3D.

After that as he painted he started to recite in rhyme the feelings that he had about that particular painting, and soon realized that he could write a poem to go with each of them. Karen was delighted and together they produced a beautiful coffee table book with the poetry on one side of the page and the painting reproduced on the other. It's been selling well, along with his many poster reproductions. He even sells his originals for thousands of dollars.

City Planner to Planning Own Home

Mustached with a twinkle in his eyes, Fred had been a City Planner with several cities in his career, all in California, but in his retirement he wanted to live near the ocean. So he and his wife bought a modest fourplex unit and started planning the home of their dreams. He had dabbled in architecture, so could design the floor plan and the elevations, so it was time to look for a lot. There was not much to choose from near the ocean, but they finally found a corner lot where a small house had been torn down and all that was left was a garage. They bought it and then started the permit process. Sixty thousand dollars later (water being the largest permit and almost denied due to dry years in the area), they broke ground. They tried to follow the latest "green" rules for a modest one-story, three bedroom, two bath home with a single car garage and drought resistant plantings. He's chosen a contractor now and is ready to build probably the most expensive but nicest home in the area.

Dancer to Producer/Director

Vivacious Lynn practiced dancing when she was young and had a career as a dancer in the chorus on Broadway in New York for much of her early years. Now over 60, she missed it and discovered some classes in Oakland, CA at StAGEbridge which she took and enjoyed so much that she was inspired to start a group where she is currently living about 80 miles away in Santa Cruz. She approached the Community College there to partner with her and to offer classes for Seniors who would like to get back into singing, dancing, acting and other "Showbiz" activities. The teachers are all professionals or teachers of the subject on the College level. Seventy seniors enrolled in the week long classes offered at the college calling it a "Senior Camp" this past summer. Now they are planning more classes in the fall and have been getting a large response to StAGEbridge (spelled this way). The founder from Oakland is working with her and expects now to go National with this idea.

CHAPTER 14
HONING YOUR SKILLS

This is your chance! Your chance to do something you enjoy.

Get yourself to seminars, talks, and lectures about subjects you have enjoyed, any related fields or new fields, because you never know until you've heard all about it whether or not it might be right for you. Go with an open mind. It may not be talking about exactly the job you had in mind for yourself, but it might be a way of getting in to that perfect job...if it relates. You also might find that you really like it better. If you don't investigate, you'll never know. You have to explore, look around and find out what's out there and what fields relate to your interests. Experiment, inquire and talk to people who are in careers that might interest you. You can make it happen, but only by having some self-confidence in yourself and your own abilities.

Then there's volunteering where the opportunities are limitless! Sometimes they can lead to a paid job, but mostly there is the satisfaction of helping others. Most cities or towns may have a Volunteer Center you can call. Where I live we have a Senior Resource Directory put out by Senior Network Services. They have a list of possible places to volunteer to help others and the community.

Love gardening?

Bright and happy, 70-year-old Kathy works as a volunteer at the Arboretum, connected with UC Santa Cruz since she has a love of gardening but now is living in a condo with no yard. She's been working there mostly with succulents. She and others make beautiful wreaths with the succulents and selling them brings money to the operation. Others like to work in the fields where they grow many varieties of plants. Then there is the store which sells starters and gifts made with plants or that are about plants. While working there, volunteers meet people from all over the world who stop by when they have been visiting or taking courses at the University.

There are other gardens in my area, one to raise money for the Homeless where volunteers help by growing things and selling them. There's another garden at a Senior Center, and there you can rent your own plot of ground to grow your food, spices or flowers. Gardening can also be a way to get great exercise!

Volunteering

Linda, an intelligent, active woman in her sixties, was an executive in a company doing high level Sales & Marketing when she met her husband, who was also an executive in another company and after they married, they seldom saw each other with all the traveling they each had to do. So they decided that "Life is too short" and that it was time to retire to a small beach town in California. While her husband was busy with Photography as a hobby, she decided to get involved as a volunteer in the small local History Museum. Today she is the President of the Board there, busy every day and loves it. At the museum they change their displays every year, so the planning is extensive and of course she had to learn about the history of the area which she found to be very exciting. She saw the museum develop from a small road house, moved from another location to its present spot, to an addition of a tiny beach cottage, typical of the early 40s, and another building housing a toilet, shower and changing house used by beach goers of the times. The main building is filled with items given by local residents from their families and sometimes even their ancestors, all having to do with history of the area. Open on weekends for tourists and Wednesdays for locals, it's manned, of course, by volunteers.

Docents

Many areas have a need for Docents, particularly in areas of National or State Parks or State Beaches and Historical sites. It takes some training, but if you are interested it's like going back to school, but learning something new about this country in which you live can be exciting. For example, our training at Seacliff State Beach took four Saturdays with guest speakers and talks by experts in Marine Biology, tours of the Visitor Center and an explanation about all the displays interpreted by the people in charge. As Docents we are required to work six hours a month which is easy to do, and most of us work more. We man the counter for sales of articles and books about our beach or show our tide pool exhibit and mention the DVD playing in the other room that tells about how this all came about. In return we each get a pass for the parking at a number of local parks and beaches for the year.

We meet together once a month for a pot luck dinner and a

talk from a Ranger or a knowledgeable person having to do with the sea and the animals around us. We learn about the other State Parks nearby so we can help visitors who are looking for other places to go to in our area. We all love what we are doing, especially when the 2nd, 4th and 6th Graders come on their field trips to visit us. We have fun and so do the youngsters, because the teachers bring them year after year. It's a win/win for everyone!

Caregiving

Caregiving, whether for a relative or another Senior, is difficult but very rewarding, according to the people who are doing it. If one is caregiving for a relative, you can often get time off with the help of local non-profit agencies who will come over to relieve you on a regular basis. In my city the Senior Network Services can help find someone, but I'm sure elsewhere there are local Non-Profits where help would be available.

And then there are people who can help Seniors in finding a new home, depending on the skills needed for their care. Names of these agencies will vary, such as "We Can Do It for You", and "A Move Made Simple", helping seniors to move to another smaller place, or "ComforCare" to help them in their own homes, with non-medical services. Others in my area are named "Visiting Angels", "Help 4 Seniors" and "Ask Barbara". All hire caregivers and prefer other Seniors who will have more in common with their clients.

More Ideas

In most fields you have to start at the bottom, so in changing careers it won't be any different even if you're mature. But I've never known a mailroom clerk to remain there for very long. They always seem to move up the ladder. Some employers will hire you at the bottom even after you have numerous college degrees, but don't be afraid to take that foot-in-the-door job in the field of your choice, because the moment another opening occurs you can move right into it. It helps to be right there when things are happening.

Especially don't be afraid of taking a cut in pay, because that is very common in changing careers. In fact, many times, it will be for no pay. You can volunteer at a non-profit, if that gives you the experience you need for later.

A good career center at a nearby college can help. They have tests you can take that will highlight your talents and interests. Yes, even at your age, you can take these tests.

Many people hate what they are doing while at work and are really looking forward to their retirement..." to do what they would like to do." Why wait? You can start now to think about it and prepare the road for that.

Can you do that now? Of course you can: it's your second 50 years!

DOREE STEINMANN

THE AUTHOR

Doree Steinmann, B.S., M.A.

Producer, Director, Editor and Host of the public community television show "Your Second Fifty Years", Doree Steinmann has produced over 500 episodes of this show over the last 25 years. She is now using this great wealth of interviews and experiences to create a book of "inspiring ideas for the second half of your life".

Doree was first heard "on-air" as radio's "Storybook Lady" which she later brought to PBS Television, where she then created an educational television show "Creative Dramatics" for middle-school students.

After years of hosting her daily TV show "Women's World" at KXTV in Sacramento, California and then becoming the first woman News Anchor in Northern California, Doree returned to education. She received her Masters Degree in Speech Communications and then created the Communications/Media curriculum at Cosumnes River College where she taught for 22 years. Teaching all the Broadcasting classes herself, she also took on the responsibility of Chairperson for the Department and was also named Faculty Senate President.

In her "retirement" Doree has served for 3 years as President of the Lifelong Learners of University of California at Santa Cruz and 8 years on the Board of Directors at Community Television of Santa Cruz County, while she continues to teach classes on "Acting for the Camera", "Interview Techniques" and "Newscasting" for middle-school students. She also continues to produce, direct, edit and host the television show "Your Second Fifty Years".

This is her first published book.

Contact Doree Steinmann through

Independent Words

Independentwords.com

www.ingramcontent.com/pod-product-compliance
Lightning Source LLC
Chambersburg PA
CBHW070542030426
42337CB00016B/2317